MORNING ROUTINE MAKEOVER

Zoe McKey is a bestselling author in the field of self-development and a communication and lifestyle coach. Visit www.zoemckey.com and get access to Zoe's Self-Discovery Starter Kit

MORNING ROUTINE MAKEOVER

Tactics and Strategies to Get More
Energized and Productive All Day

ZOE MCKEY

RUPA

Published by
Rupa Publications India Pvt. Ltd 2023
7/16, Ansari Road, Daryaganj
New Delhi 110002

Sales Centres:
Prayagraj Bengaluru Chennai
Hyderabad Jaipur Kathmandu
Kolkata Mumbai

Copyright © Zoe McKey 2023

Published under arrangement with Dorottya Zita Carlo through
TLL Literary Agency

The views and opinions expressed in this book are the author's own and the facts are as reported by him which have been verified to the extent possible, and the publishers are not in any way liable for the same.

All rights reserved.
No part of this publication may be reproduced, transmitted,
or stored in a retrieval system, in any form or by any means, electronic,
mechanical, photocopying, recording or otherwise, without the prior
permission of the publisher.

P-ISBN: 978-93-5520-949-8
E-ISBN: 978-93-5702-412-9

First impression 2023

10 9 8 7 6 5 4 3 2 1

Printed in India

This book is sold subject to the condition that it shall not, by way of
trade or otherwise, be lent, resold, hired out, or otherwise circulated,
without the publisher's prior consent, in any form of binding or
cover other than that in which it is published.

CONTENTS

Introduction		1
1.	The Circadian Rhythms	7
2.	Start Your Day with Non-Cheesy Optimism	20
3.	Set Your Self-Esteem On Track	42
4.	The Hour of Power	51
5.	Thirty Minutes For A Healthy Body and Mind	68
6.	Others' Best Practices	76
7.	Morning Nutrition and Health	84
Closing Words		99
Reference		101
Endnotes		104

INTRODUCTION

Would you like to know what my first thoughts were every morning when I woke up a few years ago?

Nothing.

Because I never woke up in the morning.

Why? The answer is simple: I worked nights. But even though I worked nights, I wanted to have good thoughts when I woke up to make something of my days, to be productive and feel energized. What does a person do when she wants to improve her habits? Buys books. Just like you did with my book, I also bought some self-help books that included morning routines people should follow to give their day the right start.

However, I was disappointed. Everywhere I read that I should wake up early at 5 a.m. or so. They said I should start my day early or it wouldn't be productive, and I wouldn't be able to reach my potential.

Okay, then why bother? I thought. I slept a few extra hours instead. The year when I worked nights, half of my daytime hours passed so uselessly that I felt like I hardly blinked before I had to go back to work again.

My daily routine looked like this: Monday through Saturday I woke up at 12 p.m., eat, watched some brain-killing TV show, went to class, took a nap in case I had to work until 5 a.m., eat, and, at 7 p.m., headed to work to get there by 8 p.m. I worked until 4 a.m., then went home and repeated the cycle. On Sundays I slept all day. Actually, counter-intuitively for most, Monday was my favorite day since it was the only day I could sleep normally at night.

You may wonder why I worked nights. I was earning my master's degree and got an ultimatum from the school. They said if I didn't start attending classes, I could kiss my degree goodbye. So I had to quit my morning job. I kept my evening one, taking on more shifts to pay my expenses.

I tell you this story to illustrate that I know what I'm talking about when I say not everyone is cut out for morning miracles. Even if I accept that the best way to have a productive day is to wake up as early as possible and do all the stuff morning routine books recommend, I understand that this only applies to people who can go to bed by 11 p.m. at the latest.

What about the rest of us? What about those who work nights, shift workers or those who are simply night owls? I thought about this every night when I could sit a little bit and contemplate about life. Since I had many nights to think, I came up with the answers. This book contains those answers. The secret how I changed my routines and as a consequence, my life in just six months.

The first part of the book will present you with everything you need to know about sleeping habits. I will present the biological background of why some people are early birds and some night owls. I will also highlight the risks of working the night shift and I provide scientifically proven tips on how to diminish the damage a twisted daily schedule can cause.

The second part of this book will present you the main exercises I did and still do every day after waking up. These exercises were my key to starting my day with a good attitude. The amazing thing is that you can practice them any time of day—the only condition is to do them after waking up. It doesn't matter if that's 5 a.m. or 5 p.m.

The third part of this book will present you the ways high achievers have of getting their day off to a great start.

The fourth part will include scientific background and useful tips for optimal after wake-up nutrition: what's good, what's bad, what's a myth, and what's a must-do.

All in all, this book is a comprehensive manual that contains everything you need to know about how to start your day in the best way possible, physiologically and mentally.

My first piece of advice to change your morning habits is to tell you not to wake up at 5 a.m. I don't think the time a person wakes is the most important contributor to productivity. It is an advantage for many people, including world-class business people, and other world leaders, but that doesn't mean it's the right solution for you.

I have studied successful people's morning routines in depth. It is true that they generally wake up early. Some out of necessity (they have to be in the office at 8 a.m. and they want to have time for themselves before their children wake up), and some because they're "early bird" types.

What about the rest of the people who are night owls? People who work in the evening or who have unpredictable work schedules? The 5 a.m. routine can not be applied in their case.

Everyone has 24 hours at their disposal. Clearly, those 24 hours can't all be productive—at least not in the long term. In Hungary there is a song with the title, "Eight hours work, eight hours rest, eight hours entertainment." It is debatable whether eight hours sleep is absolutely necessary for everybody, but for the sake of this example, I will operate with this assumption. There are 16 active hours in every 24. I have them, you have them, we all do.

The strategy I've developed emphasizes the first active hours of these 16. Regardless of when these hours start. It could be 5 a.m., 9 a.m. or 1 p.m. So they can be useful for early birds as well as night owls.

Don't worry if you usually wake up at 9 a.m. because that is the best time for you to be productive, you don't have to set an alarm for 5 a.m.

CHAPTER 1

THE CIRCADIAN RHYTHMS

Before I take you to the realm of morning habit changes, I'd like to give you a brief summary about our biological sleeping-awakening-related functions. It is essential to understand how the human body works before you start stigmatizing yourself with different labels, like you're a lazy pants in the morning or an annoying night howler. All habits have a reason and explanation that you'll be able to identify after you read this chapter.

The National Institute of General Medical Sciences defines circadian rhythms as "physical, mental, and behavioral changes that follow a roughly 24-hour cycle, responding primarily to light and darkness in an organism's environment." These changes exist in all living beings—even microbes.

Human circadian rhythms are driven by your biological clocks, which are defined by genetics. It is instinctive when you feel the need to sleep or wake up. That's why I say there is nothing weird about being a night owl or early bird– it's genetics, baby.

Circadian rhythms may be genetic, but environmental impulses also affect your sleeping patterns. Of all the external stimuli, like noise, discomfort and other disturbances, artificial light has the greatest impact on your sleep by "turning on or turning off genes that control an organism's internal clocks." In other words, if you lock yourself in a dark room at 2:00 p.m. your body will feel weird. You may fall asleep after a little while even if you are not tired. Also, if you expose yourself to light at 3:00 a.m., you'll have trouble falling asleep.

The phenomenon we call jet lag does the best job of illustrating how circadian rhythms can be modified. Jet lag happens when your circadian rhythms are interrupted. Passing through time zones, your body's clock won't keep up with your IPhones automatic time zone updates. For example, if you fly from Beijing to Los Angeles, you'll gain 15 hours. So when you're in Beijing and it is 5:00

a.m., in LA it is 2:00 p.m.

This time difference will cause total disorientation for the body. Not only for sleep but also for hunger—you're probably not so hungry at 5:00 a.m., but at 2:00 p.m., it's lunchtime. Your body will eventually adjust itself, but it takes between a few days and one week depending on how old you are and how many hours you are jumping through. Scientists say that a one-hour time difference takes one day to adjust to. I often travel from the US to Europe or vice versa. I need about four to six days to adjust to this ten-hour time difference. My sleeping habits can adjust even quicker, especially if I arrive nighttime to my destination. As told above, just a dark environment can trick your body into sleep. Interestingly, when I adjust to the new time zone I become a morning person again.

Tricking my stomach is a completely different story. It usually takes me longer to adjust my eating habits to my new time zone than my sleeping habits if I'm careless and only eat when I'm hungry—which usually is at nighttime in the local time. According to study from the University of Surrey in the U.K., if you plan to stay in your new time zone longer than two to three days, it is advisable to consciously schedule your meals according to your new time zone. So eat your breakfast when it is morning in your current location, not when is morning at home. Even if it feels like you're not hungry, try to force a few bites down your throat to survive until your next scheduled meal.

"To keep your energy levels steady, opt for lighter meals with a good balance of protein, complex carbohydrates, and plant-based foods. And make sure to have protein-rich snacks on hand, especially if you're traveling to areas where such foods are hard to find: nuts, peanut or almond butter with whole-grain bread or crackers, cheese, yogurt, or easy-to-pack protein bars," advises Amy Farley in an article of Travel+Leisure.i Other scientist advise to start to mimic the meal times of the place where you are about to go a few days—but the latest—twelve hours before. This way you'll be less affected by the negative impacts of jet lag.

Circadian rhythms impact more than just sleep cycles. They also influence bodily functions like eating time (as told in the previous paragraph), hormone releases, and body temperature regulation. If you suffer from insomnia, for example, you can ask your doctor about your circadian rhythm, the answer to your problem could be found in a related disorder. In more severe cases an abnormal circadian rhythm can lead to depression, obesity, or diabetes. If experience any of these problems, ask your doctor to run some tests to identify if your issues are connected with circadian rhythm abnormalities. Do not search for answers on the Internet or in this book.

HOW CAN CIRCADIAN RHYTHMS AFFECT OUR DAILY MORNING ROUTINES?

Circadian rhythms determine your sleep patterns. A hormone called melatonin makes you feel sleepy. Your body's "master clock" is responsible for controlling this hormone. This master clock (also called the Suprachiasmatic Nucleus or SCN) is a group of cells in the hypothalamus located close to your optic nerves. When the optic nerves get the message about light or darkness through your eyes, the master clock is affected.

If it senses darkness, it sends melatonin that makes you sleep and reduces your body temperature. If it senses light, it will withdraw this hormone and you'll have trouble falling asleep.

Humans are considered to be diurnal. This means that, unlike nocturnal animals that are active at night, we are naturally more active during the day. The right time for sleeping for us is in the night portion of our circadian rhythm. Biologically speaking our lowest body temperature and highest melatonin level should happen around the end of our sleep session. Studies have shown that in most cases core body temperature is lowest and melatonin level is highest at around 5 a.m. Soon afterward the body sends signals to wake up. It's also important to mention that melatonin starts to spread in an adult body around 8 or 9 p.m., and stops between 7 a.m. and 8 a.m. During the day, in normal cases, melatonin should be absent from the human body.

WHAT'S THE DIFFERENCE BETWEEN "EARLY BIRDS" AND "NIGHT OWLS?"

An individual's chronotype indicates the time of day when a person is physically more active. Circadian rhythms can be adjusted by up to two hours either way. Some of us tend to wake up early and are most alert—mentally and physically—early in the day. Others are more alert in the late evening and tend to go to bed late.

Researchers have proved that around 20 percent of the population falls into one category or the other—early birds or night owls. The rest have the more general circadian rhythm. Because of their genes, morning and evening people have tilted circadian periods. In other words, morning people wake up at a later stage in their circadian cycle. Thus they are much more alert upon waking. Evening people wake up too early in their circadian cycle. Therefore, they are less alert when they wake. Normally this shift in circadian rhythm is only a few hours earlier or later than average. For somebody that has a shifted circadian rhythm, it can be really difficult to work or go to school for regular 9 a.m. to 5 p.m. hours.

WHAT ABOUT NIGHT SHIFT WORKERS?

Night shift work became popular in the second half of the 19th century when electricity became wide spread. People could be kept in factories to work day and night. Shift work affected 20-25 percent of the working class and with the advent of Henry Ford's assembly line this percentage increased considerably.

If you work two or three night shifts, your biological clock can become seriously twisted and this can effect your sleep because you expose your body to light when your circadian rhythm expects darkness, and vice versa. Even after years of work, your body won't adapt to these kinds of shifts.

The body needs one day to adapt to a one-hour difference.[2] So imagine if you go to work from 8 a.m. until 8 p.m. then the next week from 8 p.m. to 8 a.m. That kind of adjustment would require twelve days. Working three shifts or rotating shifts (for example from 8 a.m. to 4 p.m., 4 p.m. to 12 a.m., and 12 a.m. to 8 a.m. changing every week for three weeks) is even worse than a regular night shift because your circadian rhythm will never have time to adjust even for a little while.

If you work on a regular night shift, you may get about two hours less sleep than the average person. The loss of these sleep hours is not caused by a circadian rhythm disorders, but by the social engagement and pressure you feel to be active during the daytime with your family and friends.

When I worked nights I hardly ever had time for my friends and family because I was always so tired. Sometimes I met people, but I was often moody, tired, and even angry with them for their simple existence. (*How can they be so inconsiderate? They make me sit in this noisy café instead of letting me sleep!*) After a while nobody was interested in meeting me. I was the grumpy zombie. I felt socially isolated so I made an effort, I woke up and drank a zillion of energy drinks to keep me awake for my social engagements, but that hijacked my health. After that I was not only exhausted and tired zombie, but also a sick one. My memory started playing funny games with me, I had trouble focusing, I did poorly on my exams, and I became highly unmotivated at work.

Studies proved that people who work nights can experience fatigue, poor memory recall and performance, gastrointestinal problems, and other unpleasantness. In more severe cases, when they worked night shifts for years, chronic fatigue, cardiovascular disorders, depression, diabetes, ulcers, and some forms of cancer sometimes affected them as well.

It's an interesting, although not surprising fact that many big industrial and transportation catastrophes like Exxon Valdez, Chernobyl, or Three Mile Island happened at night. Studies show that the risk of accidents is estimated to be about 30 percent greater during nighttime than daytime shifts. This percentage can increase with the length of shifts and the number of consecutive nights the workers worked.

There are, however, some ways to reduce the negative effect of shift or night work. Making workplace lights similar to natural light can be a good start to reduce the negative effect of shift work. Increasing the intensity and changing the wavelength of light toward the blue end of the spectrum can help workers adapt to working at night. Even their ability to sleep during the day may get better.

You can try to trick your body's biological clock into thinking it's nighttime by wearing dark glasses when returning home in the morning. (Use darkened glasses that still allow you clarity of vision. Don't drive with glasses used to see an eclipse.) If you limit after-work, pre-sleep exposure to light, you can increase the positive effects of the trick.

Coffee is not always unhealthy. Use it strategically to help you stay awake. Consume caffeine regularly in small doses rather than in infrequent large doses. Stop caffeine consumption halfway through your shift so you body's caffeine level can decline before you need to sleep.

Take short breaks for 20-30 minute naps at work. It has been shown that taking naps improves night shift performance.

Understanding how the body's internal clock functions can help you handle a lot of frustrations you may feel, like why you struggle more at a night or why you hate waking up in the morning. These habits may have nothing to do with stamina or weakness. It simply means that you're strongest mental activity is not in the morning or evening. If you have a morning job being a night owl you'll constantly feel inadequate. Just like having an afternoon job being an early bird.

I had hard time accepting that I am a morning person. In college, classmates and roommates used to mock me because it was uncool to go to bed as early as I did. Do not let yourself be bullied. Don't feel bad about how your body works.

Knowing how your body's clock functions can help you choose what kind of work is fitting for you. For example, if you know you are more of an evening person, you may struggle if you work at a bed and breakfast because you'd have to wake up at 4 a.m. every day. Or, if you're a morning person, don't choose to work at a nightclub. Catering may work better. If feel tired or out of rhythm with your work, you'll probably hate it. How could you do an honest, optimist morning routine if you hate doing whatever follows? If you feel your work makes you unhappy because the hours you work are unnatural for you, think about making a change. If you don't, working the wrong hours may, in the long run, ruin your mood and your health.

SUMMARY OF CHAPTER 1

1. Circadian rhythms "are physical, mental, and behavioral changes that follow a roughly 24-hour cycle, responding primarily to light and darkness in an organism's environment."

2. Circadian rhythms, not only regulate sleep cycles, they influence many more body functions like hormone release, eating habits and body temperature.

3. Morning people wake up at a later stage in their circadian day. Thus they are much more alert upon waking. Evening people wake up early in their circadian day. Therefore, they are less alert upon waking.

CHAPTER 2

START YOUR DAY WITH NON-CHEESY OPTIMISM

THE HAPPINESS TRAP

Pursuing happiness is one of the major goals in our lives. We chase the end of the rainbow all the time. Sometimes we're so preoccupied with finding happiness that we fail to notice the moments when we *are* happy. We catch up only when the moment becomes a memory. We're more likely to observe our lack of happiness than its presence. Why?

Because "losses loom larger than gains" (Kahneman & Tversky, 1979).

Psychologically speaking, it is suggested that the pain of losing something is about twice as powerful as the pleasure of getting. Given this observation, it is not hard to see why moments of happiness are less powerful than moments of loss. For example, if you're wishing for a car and you get it, you'll feel a positive emotion half as powerful as the negative emotion you'd feel if the car was stolen.

Kahneman states that people are more likely to overestimate the happiness they're about to feel when they get something and underestimate the pain they will feel if they lose it. The saying, "You don't know what you've got 'til it's gone" is popular for a reason. To me, all this adds up to one conclusion: We don't really know what makes us happy and what doesn't.

Getting stuck in the realm of expectations and perceived best ways for happiness, therefore, is not only emotionally crippling, but also fickle. Even if we achieve our desired happiness, chances are that it won't make us as happy as we hoped for. Certainly, it won't make up for the tons of nerves we frayed along our bumpy road to get it.

When you try to hold water in your hands and you tighten your fist too hard, water will flow out. The same goes for happiness; if you try to be happy too hard, you won't be. Not long ago, I started questioning the effectiveness of "positive thinking" or "positivism." In all the books I read, it was said that positive thinking is the key to happiness. But how can we know what the key to happiness is when we can't be sure how happy something will make us?

I was puzzled. I started questioning beliefs that previously made so much sense to me. As I studied more and more about the nature of emotions, I realized that happiness, just like other basic emotions, happens unconsciously. For example, when you're angry, you don't know you're angry. You just feel angry. You don't have an inner monologue like, "Behold, World, how angry I am." You live the anger unconsciously in the moment, and later it will be gone. Just like people with high self-esteem don't wonder whether or not they have high self-esteem, happy people don't wonder whether or not they are happy. They just are.

This led me to another thought. You don't become

angry just because you want to be angry. Anger has to be triggered by some external stimuli. The same goes for happiness—it is the byproduct of a series of events in life.

The words "positivism" and "happiness" are not synonyms. If you have a friend who always seems cheerful and positive regardless of the circumstances, he or she has probably the most dysfunctional mindset of all the people you know. Trying to deny negative emotions will actually highlight those emotions and extend their length. How good it is to say "everything is okay" while your house is burning around you? Negative emotions are not an obstacle to happiness. They are needed to feel profound happiness.

While a positive mindset is not a bad thing, it has to be controlled, and definitely shouldn't be considered as the cure for negative emotions.

I consciously used the word "optimism" instead of any version of the word "positive" in the chapter title. I do not want you to expect that this book is about the general "benefits" of positivism—namely that people who practice it will be happier, healthier, more successful, kinder, they will live longer, and so on. Being optimistic and hoping for the best of your circumstances and people around you leads to successful performance during your day. Optimism doesn't push you to expect the aforementioned fluff of positive thinking.

Studies have proven that people's performance rises to the level of their expectations. Therefore, if you have optimistic mindset about your performance (even if this means overestimating your potential), research suggests that you're more likely to achieve your goal than if you're neutral or negative. A pinch of healthy delusion never caused world wars.

Optimists are more likely to believe something is good when in reality, it is bad. Pessimists will believe something is bad when it's actually good. Unless the perceived goods and bads are not extreme, it can be concluded that optimism serves you much better than pessimism. Let's use an example of this extreme to avoid confusion here: If someone thinks about genocide as good, even though it is bad, that's not optimism. That's madness.

Why is optimism better? Because it makes people more open to saying yes to things. Sometimes they might say yes to the dullest things, but their chances are high to mine out some real gems from the ashes of dullness, while pessimists will bury the diamonds in the ashes even if they are holding the diamonds directly in their palms.

Based on science and my own experience, I can tell you with peace of mind that an optimistic attitude is much better to have in the mornings, and in general.

You might wonder why I distinguish the words "optimistic" and "positive." Although dictionaries are not helpful to make a clear distinction between these two words, I still think there is a difference in their meaning. A person is an optimist when he or she is hopeful about the future and certain situation. When someone is positive, it is more of a habit of character, and for that matter, an unnatural state of being. It is more difficult to be positive than to be optimistic. In my understanding, positive people are generally optimistic, but optimistic people don't necessarily have to be positive. For example, when I was working two jobs at sixteen hours a day, I was a very negative person. Still, I felt I was lucky to have two jobs, as some people struggle to have one. I also believed that my future would be brighter. I was not positive at all, but I was optimistic.

Words have a strange power over the mind. That's why I chose to use the word "optimistic" instead of "positive" when it comes to morning routines. A switch to an optimistic lifestyle can be accomplished much easier and quicker than a switch to positivity.

IMPROVE YOUR OPTIMISTIC PRIMING

Optimistic priming is very similar to positive affirmations, except that you don't have to repeat them in front of the mirror one hundred times. You don't have to hug the love-tree three times a day and walk around it starting with your left foot. You don't need heart-shaped Post-Its around your room telling that you're a wonderful person (which you are). You need, however, to rewire your brain and gently force it to think differently.

Changing your thoughts is the best chance you've got for an energetic morning, and as a matter of fact, a happy life.

Choose the optimistic priming of having a good day as a mantra, no matter what. Your hair is messy? Your day still will be beautiful. You feel all moody and gloomy? Your day still will be good. Optimistic priming increases your chances for success.

No pillow-drama-death today. Get rid of your good old pessimistic knee-jerk reactions. Question them as simply as this may sound. *"Is it really true that a sloppy head has any kind of effect on my day?"* Negative and pessimistic thoughts invade the mind like a horde of Mongols only because we accept them as unconditional truth.

If you wake up with a melancholic mood, try to question your negative thoughts first instead of coming up with optimistic ones that you can't really relate to. *"Is it really a bad day?"* or *"Am I really tired, or do I just not want to go to work?"* Identify what really troubles your mind and find an optimistic priming method regarding that issue. "Today will be an amazing day" is a very good mantra to have, but if you're looking forward for a life-or-death operation, it will seem rather unhelpful. But if you say, "Today, the surgery will be the greatest success in all medical history," you'll channel a more specific kind of optimism.

Don't feel guilty for thinking about negative things most of the time. It doesn't mean there's something's wrong with you. In fact, if you never had any negative thoughts, it would mean that something was not okay between your ears. Negative expectations mean you're human. People are genetically coded to have negative thoughts ever since we climbed down from the trees. The evolution of the brain is responsible for your worrying, stressing, angry persona. Our emotional brain is millions of years older than our thinking brain. The emotional brain was responsible for our ancestors' survival. Without a genuinely suspicious and negatively wired emotional brain, our species would be pretty much extinct today. If the homo habilis cheerfully hummed on the mountain top all day instead of staying on guard to protect themselves from a T-Rex, another homo habilis, or the changeable environment, their lives could have met a bitter end at any moment. They had to stay alert and always expect the worst.

Their fight-or-flight response never left us millennials

now running around with smartphones and organic chia seed drinks. Evolution couldn't catch up with the accelerated development of the human society; therefore, deep down in our emotional brain (limbic system), we're still Flintstones fighting for survival, even though the chances that our lives are indeed threatened are minimal.

Waking up with a bunch of negative ants running up and down on the wires of your brain is natural. It doesn't mean, however, that you have to stick with them. You can't change how you feel most of the time, but you can alter your thoughts.

Whatever your mood might be, close your eyes. Take some deep breaths, give in to the amazing feeling of being alive. Feel the oxygen filling your lungs. Be thankful for it. Imagine that it is evening, and the day went on exactly as you imagined. You nailed the promotion, your surgery was a success, and you even got ice cream after, or your day simply passed in harmony with your loved ones. Take a deep breath while you repeat imagining these pictures. Inhale. Fill your lungs with air as you count to four. Then hold the fresh air in your body for three to four seconds. Feel that you are alive—feel that gentle, numb feeling in your palms, your arms, your face, and chest. Exhale slowly; let out all your fears and unrealistically negative thoughts with your exhalation. Then inhale again with the air of hope and optimism.

You are alive. You can move, read, think, and thus, appreciate. Today, you'll have a fantastic day. Today, you'll have a successful presentation. Today, you'll find the best pet in the shelter. Today, you'll perform at your best. Why? Because there is no reason why it would happen otherwise. Focus on what you have, not what you lack. "Trade your expectations for appreciation," said Tony Robbins. If you do so, there will be no room for dissatisfaction, sorrow, and unhappiness.

The exercise of optimistic priming shouldn't take more than three to five minutes.

A few years ago, I found the exercise of optimistic priming quite unnecessary, even stupid. When I decided to consciously change my morning routines, I read and tried several practices that didn't help me much—including the practice of positive affirmations. I was full of expectations, and I expected these methods to work instantly. Every time I bought a self-help book, I believed that now was the moment of permanent change. After reading them, I got inspired, swept up in a fake feeling of glory and success before even doing anything. I started doing the practices enthusiastically. If you ever wondered who's the person doing the exercises recommended in a book, I was them.

I really needed change in my life a few years ago, because it was getting out of my control. I had two jobs—one from 9 a.m. to 6 p.m. and the other from 8 p.m. to 4 a.m. I felt overwhelmed by work, fatigue, sleeplessness, and warnings from my university that if I skipped any more classes I'll be expelled.

I was desperately wishing for a Harry Potter - like time machine so I can go back in time and accomplish multiple things happening at the same time like Hermione! After a few days unsuccessfully wishing for an imaginary device I turned my attention to more realistic objectives. Since I know I can't have more hours in a day, I shifted my focus to having more energy.

I started reading about energizing daily habits—

morning habits included. I read so many self-help books I can't count. Tony Robbins, Oprah, and others. I got into a vicious spiral of repetitive reading. You know, the same thing happens when you go to a productivity seminar and you feel very productive but in fact you're not productive at all. You just sit and listen to another guy talking about productivity but nothing changes in your life. I fell into the productivity seminar trap—this is how I used to call it. I read about becoming more positive but I never actually became positive. I did the exercises but never actually could relate with them. I also fell into the mistake of excess—I wanted to implement everything I read in ten books immediately in my life without even considering that the exercise can't even fit my uncommon schedule.

My enthusiasm quickly dropped. After a few days I grew tired of the many changes in my life. I felt everything unnatural and lost my motivation. I started feeling guilt for getting defeated so easily so quickly so I bought another book and started everything all over again. In a few days I ended up at the same place as before. No. I ended up even lower. Every failed attempt to turn my sinking ship around proved me more and more that my negative beliefs are true.

Regardless of how often I told the mirror how much I loved myself, exercised for 30 minutes, read or listened to a motivational speech where the guy told me to be happy after he'd clearly had more hours of sleep than I had, and meditated on the tram so I wouldn't be late for work or class I hated my life. My meditation sessions on the tram were often so successful that the driver had to kick me off at the final station because I looked like a homeless person sleeping in my PJ pants that I forgot to change in my morning rush. I felt like a pathetic, tired loser who is so inferior to those amazing people who give these sensible positive thinking advice while they sip their asparagus smoothie on their private island somewhere in Indonesia.

Long story short—I became devastated instead of motivated. The remorse felt when I skipped something was the worst part of this entire circus. It didn't take me too much time to realize that my compulsive attempts to be positive did me more harm than good. I felt I had enough. I tossed my self-help collection into a box and pushed it onto the top shelf of my wardrobe. I even closed the door so those little traitors couldn't peek and see how I'd fallen back into my bad habits.

Why did I open Pandora's box and see the promise of a better life, which I couldn't reach? What is wrong with me?

One day I woke up on a beautiful Sunday afternoon. Birds were tweeting, the sun was shining and I still had some leftover pizza. "What else do I need?" I thought. "I could finally sleep, now I can eat." I opened the door on my balcony and if I was a Disney princess, I would have started singing to the birds. My unusual happy mood made me suspicious first. Something must be wrong with me. Maybe I'm going crazy. As I sat on my balcony thinking about my mood swing, the answer came out of the blue.

I was full of positive expectations. But expectations are still expectations, regardless of their nature. Adding up all the positive expectations ends in a negative result. I overestimated my adaptability. I wanted instant change, now now now. When my expectations weren't met I got pissed. Do you remember how disappointed you've got as a child when you wanted the fairy Barbie for Christmas but you only got socks and panties? I was dwelling in the same childish rage when I didn't get my instant gratification for my reading efforts.

On that Sunday morning, on the other hand I didn't have any expectations. I was just simply grateful. Grateful for the sun, for enough sleep and half rotten pizza. Zero expectations.

The problem with positive thinking and positive affirmations is that involuntarily, we associate expectations to them. As soon as we start practicing something, or repeating something, we accept it as real. But if things don't turn out as we expected them to, we become disappointed.

At a higher level of self-awareness, people can prescind if their positive affirmations don't always bring the expected results. But at the beginning of a self-improvement journey, you're just not there yet. That is a challenge that requires skills on level ten, but right now, you're on level one. And when I say you, I mean me. At that moment, I was at level one. I was negative, whiny, with zero self-awareness. The only thing I could cling to were the things I already had.

Things you have are secure subjects for gratitude, and as a consequence, a good day. Things you can be grateful for are already yours—they don't depend on your future actions.

Instead of humming positive affirmations, simply be grateful when you wake up. Instead of having a rock-solid mantra, choose your optimistic priming sentence based on what are you about to face today. In my opinion, these are the basics of a successful morning routine. Everything else is a next-level exercise.

KNOW YOUR WHYS

Apart of knowing what you want to accomplish using optimistic priming, it is also important to know why you want to use it. Some people don't really know why they do things—they just do them.

My friend, for example, goes to kung fu classes

regularly although she claims she hates it. One day I asked her the million-dollar question: why do you do kung fu? She was all shoulder shrugs. She didn't know. She said she doesn't feel passionate about it. She hates that kung fu is repetitive. She finds that boring. Then I asked her why she chose such a repetitive physical exercising form as martial arts? They are all about repetition so the motions burn into the body and mind and become reflexes when they are needed.

Then she confessed that she knows her dad always wanted a son, and that her boyfriend is into martial arts—he also does kung fu. She convinced herself that she wanted to do it, too. Fear of rejection pushed her to continue a routine she hated.

You can't be positive about something you hate. You just can't. There is no magic formula that can cure that problem. People may watch a touching movie, read an inspiring book, or talk to somebody who bewitches and inspires them, someone who has such a powerful influence that they start pursuing something they don't really want. And, years later, they find themselves full of regrets because they spent their lives following someone else's ideas instead of their own.

Don't fall in the trap of not knowing your whys when doing something, or knowing that your whys are actually someone else's whys, yet still doing what you do as if it was your preferred choice.

You want to earn money but you're too ashamed to admit it? You want to become a freelancer but you're terrified what might others say? There's nothing wrong with wanting more money, or wanting to live a free life without restriction, or to get as many degrees as possible. Just make sure that is what you really want.

Don't forget the "something for something" rule. If you want to become rich, you inevitably have to sacrifice other things - usually a lot of free time. You have to say no to many adventures, invitations, and expenditures if you want to grow your wallet.

If you want to live a carefree life you can always teach surfing and braid bracelets on a sunshine-kissed Caribbean shore, but don't count on getting fabulously wealthy.

Honesty is key in identifying your "whys." People—

just like my kung fu friend—often convince themselves they want things just because those things are highly appreciated in our society. Or, on the contrary, they reject things because society thinks less of them.

There are some behavior patterns that are universally recognized and admired, like helping people in need. We can agree that this is something to be admired in a person—the willingness to help. But, there's a twist.

Let's say you have a well-paid job. If you want to help protect the endangered lynx from extinction, the best thing for you to do is not to do the fieldwork yourself, placing 10 feeders with food, but to hire fifty people to do the work more efficiently so they'll be able to place 500 feeders with food. Unless your aim is to *look* charitable instead of *being* charitable. If this is the case, it's fine too. Just admit it so you can find your own best reasons to wake up.

Don't get me wrong. I'm not saying there's a minimum standard one should hit to be charitable. If you only have the opportunity to give only 50$ for the WWF to save lynx because you hardly make ends meet, that's more than praise worthy. There is never too little you could do for a noble cause. Just be certain what your core motivations are.

Whatever your "why" is, admit and accept it fully. You are not wrong when you honestly accept who you are and what your motivations are. Publius Terentius Afer said, "I am human, I consider nothing human alien to me." If it was true in 170 BC, why wouldn't it be true today?

Maybe your goal is to be famous, or maybe it's to influence people's lives, or to be well-informed about world affairs. Whatever it is, admit it. This knowledge and acceptance will give you a clarity of mind, a new motivation to wake up for and relieves you from the sense of confusion you felt until you didn't know why you did certain things.

A clear purpose in life starts with a "what" and a "why"—just as written above, and goes on with the "how." I talk more about this in the next chapter.

SUMMARY OF CHAPTER 2

1. No permanent change can be made instantly.
2. Set your optimistic priming in accordance with your daily tasks.
3. Trade expectations for appreciation.
4. Start your day with the sentence that empowers your greatest hope for that day.
5. Why do you want what you want for that day?
6. Wake up every morning with a clear purpose in your life.

CHAPTER 3

SET YOUR SELF-ESTEEM ON TRACK

Practicing optimistic priming is a way of taking care of yourself. The more you keep to this routine, the more satisfied you'll feel. The more satisfied you are and the more you'll love yourself. Ultimately you'll feel better in your own skin without even noticing it. There is, however, another important aspect to consider before becoming overly optimistic, namely staying realistic in your optimism. It sounds counterintuitive but the two concepts are not mutually exclusive.

Don't promise yourself too much with your optimistic priming. For example, if you buy a lottery ticket, don't take for granted that you will win. The odds are very high that you won't. I don't want to be a killjoy if you bought lottery tickets before you purchased this book, but there's a one in a million (or more) chance for picking the lucky numbers. If you base your optimism on sandcastles that always collapse, sooner or later, you'll lose your optimistic attitude. You'll also lose some self-respect. As a consequence, you'll feel remorse, and you'll be angry with the person who misled you—yourself.

Think about how you feel about those people who kept promising things to you and failed to deliver them. Recall how much resentment you felt when someone constantly promised you optimistic results and because of lack of rational thinking or simple sloth didn't deliver you any kind of result. Why would you intentionally bring this kind of self-resentment upon yourself?

Start things simple. Respect yourself, start small, and as your optimistic priming sessions bring good results, raise the stakes. First, be optimistic about getting the chance to work out for thirty minutes instead of running the marathon tomorrow.

No one but you can be blamed for what you're doing, and how you live. Whether or not you change your morning thoughts is up to you. Your success or failure will be your responsibility. It is easier to blame others for your failures. Many people do that. And these people rarely fulfill their dreams. They are busy inventing excuses about why they didn't succeed instead of focusing on improvement and achievement.

If there is one mantra you wish to repeat like a good student, or put on a post-it above your head should sound somehow like this:

I take responsibility for my own life. I am able to cope with any situation! I am resilient. I will earn success!

HELP YOUR SELF-ESTEEM

Poor self-esteem can be caused by not noticing confirmations and rarely by the lack of them. Usually there are positive feedbacks around us we just don't pay attention on them.

People's perceived happiness often depends on what others say or think about them. This reflects very well in Facebook's liking system. If you get likes for your photo temporarily you'll feel good about yourself. If you don't get the expected feedback, you'll feel unloved, uninteresting, and rejected.

It is easy to become dependent to social media because it gives positive feedback easily. However, its honesty is questionable. Besides it is just as easy to get negative feedback or lack of feedback that has a negative effect. People give too much credit to social media platforms. They post a picture of their scrambled eggs. Then they cling to their profile all day to see how many people liked their post. If they get fifty likes for their scrambled eggs they feel relieved.

Good. Good. I'm cool, I'm likable, right? I got fifty likes, I'm likable.

However if they don't get any feedback, or only their mother likes the post, they feel awful.

I knew it. Nobody cares about my scrambled eggs. They hate me. I'm ignored totally. I should have posted a different picture. I'll try another picture later. It has to be later so everyone doesn't think that I live on Facebook. But look at this! My friend got one hundred likes on her hamburgers. Why? Why is her hamburger better than my scrambled eggs?

Isn't this mental paralysis insane? True self-esteem comes from internal reassurance. You are responsible only for your own fate and thoughts. You may only decide for yourself and can't control other people's decisions. You can't make someone else love, accept, or like you.

Know what you want, and make decisions to the best of your ability to achieve your goals. If your happiness depends on someone else's feedback, you will never truly be free and satisfied. The key is to find happiness in yourself.

You'd be surprised how much good feedback you get every day that you choose to ignore because your self-esteem can't identify it. If you think low about yourself, praise will seem like a lie to you, but you'll never miss an occasion to accept criticism. Why? Because they resonate with your inner world, even if they are not true.

Take the time to notice how much love and trust you get and how many look after you for a change. Life gives you what you think of yourself. You have to consider yourself worthy to get the things you desire.

This is not easy. Especially if you deeply resent yourself. But you can change it. You're opened to create better morning habits; you want to live a better life. You know that optimistic priming on a realistic ground can help you have a better day. You also know that appreciation can eliminate the pain expectations cause in your life. Practicing these two little mental switches can improve your mornings significantly. When you practice these exercises without focusing on them means that they've become a habit. It means you've mastered level one in the proverbial scale of self-development mastery. You have the basics. Then and only then should you move on to the next step.

REWRITE THE STORY YOU TELL YOURSELF

The proverbial level two of self-development mastery is to change the story you tell yourself. That's not an easy task. You tell yourself the story that brought you to the situation you live today for a long time. You rehearsed it well. Like an old actor who played the *Phantom of the Opera* at least five hundred times in his life. If he woke him in his sleep, he'd still knew his part fluently. Here are some examples of "stories" we tell ourselves:

- I won't quit my job because I can't do anything else,
- I'm not good enough to write a book,
- I don't deserve this position,
- Why should I, above all people, be selected to do it—I never was a good leader,
- And I don't have good communication skills etc.

These are all beliefs that limit self-development. I have some good news; you can stop them anytime. Just start telling yourself other stories. Switch your pessimistic stories to optimistic, reassuring sentences. It will take you time to truly believe them. The longer you lived in the negative, the longer the readjustment will be. You can't realistically expect to rewrite a twenty-year-old story after a few attempts. If you played the Phantom of the Opera for a quarter of a century, it will take you some time to learn the role of *Jesus Christ, Superstar* just as well.

Change the previous, pessimistic sentences like this:

- I can do anything I put my mind to, therefore if I want a new job I can create the background for it,
- I have all the skills needed to write a book,
- I deserve this position, I deserve the best of everything,
- I, above all people, should be selected to do it—I can face every situation,
- and I have good communication skills etc.

The more often you rehearse the new role, the deeper it will get under your skin. If you feel the need, write down the transcript of your pessimistic beliefs. First, observe what are those negative "stories" you tell yourself. Then put their antidotes on a paper, record them on your phone and read them, or listen to them as many times a day as necessary. The frequency of practice can accelerate the process of rewiring your thoughts.

SUMMARY OF CHAPTER 3:

1. I respect myself. I start small with my optimistic priming and I'll stay on the land of rationality.

2. I take responsibility for my own life. I am able to cope with any situation! I am resilient. I will earn success!

3. I notice how much love and trust I get and how many look after me.

4. I am worthy of all that life can offer.

5. I commit to rewrite the pessimistic stories in my head to optimistic ones.

CHAPTER 4

THE HOUR OF POWER

The exercise I'm about to present is not an everyday exercise. How useful or interesting you find it, or if you like it, will determine how often you feel the need to do it. You can practice it every day, if you have the time and willingness. But it can still bring good results if you do it only once a week or a month. What matters is to practice it on your chosen consistency, if you commit to it.

The first time I heard about the concept of the Hour of Power was not Tony Robbins' success seminar, or a weightlifting commercial. I heard it when I was working as a translator at an insurance company.

Every Wednesday afternoon this branch scheduled an hour of intensive cooperation work for their employees.

The main goal was to gather everybody in the same room and make client calls in front of each other to serve as a positive (or negative) example and provide extra knowledge and motivation for all employees. The purpose was learning in practice. The less successful people on the team could see first-hand how a high achiever talks, pauses, how often they make a joke, and so on. They wanted each person to see the best practices in action, to become inspired, and to keep them competitive, to see that even shy John can nail it, so it's not impossible for anyone.

I was inspired by this exercise. People can be reluctant at first to expose themselves in public—especially at work. They may fear judgment or becoming the laughing stock of others. However, since it was a work requirement, the agents couldn't escape. They had to do the calls. I could observe the improvement on the agents' sales technique week by week. At first everybody felt awkward, their voices were shaky, they were overcautious with their language, but as the sessions went on they got more comfortable around each other. Those who didn't do as well started using the style and language of the more successful agents, and they increased their own sales.

As time passed, the agents adapted the technique of their colleagues to suit themselves and found their own successful sales formulas. A few months after the first session, the agency turned into a similar circus as the one we saw in the movie *The Wolf of Wall Street*—but insurance edition. Everyone was on their phones, screaming, whispering, joking, scaring the soul out of the client—and nailing the deal.

This practice helped both the weaker agents and the successful ones, too. The achievers saw how others imitated them. This filled them with a sense of importance, confidence and they pushed themselves twice as hard to not get caught up on. They became more confident in their technique. Soon started taking on the role of helper and teacher to the weaker agents to help them improve. By teaching they also learned a lot about themselves, their presentation skills. Based on the feedbacks they got, they could improve their own techniques.

Long story short, the Hour of Power session was a win-win for the employees, for the company, and also for the customers since they heard shorter, more thoughtful and thorough presentations made by more-knowledgeable agents. The "Hour of Power branch" grew from being nowhere to becoming one of the top three agencies in the country.

Why did I tell you this story and how does it relate to morning routines? It contains important elements you can use in your improved morning routines.

As I said, you can choose the frequency of practice of the exercise I'm just about to present. I'd like to emphasize that you don't have to do it for an entire hour, even if the name of the practice might imply it. The main point is not how long your session lasts, but how much effort and how many good and constructive ideas you put into it. So if you only have ten, fifteen, or thirty minutes to do it, that's fine too. Anything is better than nothing, and the last thing you want good habits to do is stress you out.

Did you know that in the United States the greatest endemic is anxiety? People are so stressed out. They are always in a rush, eat whether they are hungry, whether not, drink coffee like a hippo drinks water, listen to loud music, and rely on other mood boosters to keep themselves up with the accelerated 21st century. Studies show that people of the United States make up 5 percent of the global population but consume 80 percent of the world's cocaine for example.

Why is this so? Some of the main reasons are the lack of gratitude and expectations blown out of proportion. If people don't appreciate what they have, they become unhappy, even when they are fortunate. Trade your expectations for appreciation.

People feel like they don't have enough. They focus on things they don't have instead of being grateful for what they do have. It is not difficult to fill books with the stuff we don't have—especially today. There are so many options, places to go, things to buy, that even if we had unlimited money and time, it would take centuries to try them all.

This is a serious issue. Problems generated by the paradox of choice are first world problem on one hand, but a borderline Western epidemic on the other hand.

These problems are powerful enough to push people to sniff a bit of coke, to drink a cocktail or ten, and to swallow a bullet in extreme cases.

Gratitude is truly missing from today's society. Thankfulness for the amazing things people have.

There is no situation where you can't find a little bit of good, something to be grateful for. If you have a hated job, try to see your situation like this: "It's so great that I have a job! Some people struggle to get one." If you ended up on the street, try this "I'm grateful that the sun is shining today, it could be raining." If you're a soldier who is at war, "I opened my eyes today, I'm alive. I'm a day closer to embrace my family, I woke up naturally, not to the sound of bombs falling."

My mother always impresses me. She's had an incurable disease for almost twenty years. This illness disfigured her body and twisted her mind, but she can still laugh, hope, and give thanks even though she has much less than many people. It truly inspires me to go forward and to never give up—for her sake as well as my own.

Gratitude empowers. Gratitude releases you from stress, sorrow and bitterness.

My version of the Hour of Power (HOP) focuses on jamming as much gratitude as possible into your life. You can do this practice in two ways:

1. The Hour of Power as a group activity (inspired by the experience I had at my workplace presented in this chapter).
2. The Hour of Power as an individual activity (inspired by Tony Robbins' morning routine technique).

1. THE HOUR OF POWER AS A GROUP ACTIVITY

The main points of the HOP group activity:

a) It is a group activity where people can see and hear each other working toward the common goal.
b) The exercise breaks the barriers of shame, intimidation, and fear. It creates the possibility to learn from each other.

c) For those who didn't have a good sales technique, the exercise was a great possibility for improvement. For those who had a good technique, it was useful to fill in their gaps and improve.

My version fitting for a morning routine version is the following: gather at least one or two friends, your partner, your parents, your kids, whoever you want, and agree that on specific time (once a week, a month etc.) you will do an HOP session together. Remember, it doesn't have to actually last one hour—but it can. You can do it any time. You can all wake up a little bit earlier than usual and have a Skype conference (if you're not living in the same household). You can schedule a twenty-minute session on your lunch break with two colleagues every Thursday. Be creative.

THE CONTENT OF THE SESSION:

The Hour of Power doesn't have to consist purely of talking about gratitude, but you should definitely save at least five to ten minutes for it. The other part of the

HOP can be about whatever you or your peers need help with. For example: a presentation coming up, parenting skills, how to be happier, how to declutter your mind or environment—general life improvement topics.

It's up to you. The only purpose of the exercise is to practice gratitude and to collect solutions for issues that give you headache. There is no good or bad topic to talk about. Everything that can help you wake up your brain and put it to work on solutions instead of problems can useful. Be careful not to turn the HOP session into a gossip or complaining session. If there is a problem you seek solutions for—for example, how to parent you fourteen-year-old who started wearing weird makeup and you suspect she's smoking—summarize the issue shortly, and then focus on solutions, best parenting practices, and so on. Don't forget to be grateful that you have a child who is just acting as a normal teenager, and who is healthy and a good kid otherwise.

Stay on the sunny side. For example, brainstorm about how to achieve something, not about how to avoid something.

Don't get discouraged if you can't find a common goal to talk about right away, or if the session starts a bit oddly. For example, maybe you want to talk about enhancing happiness in your life, but your talking partner would rather talk about improving their dating life. That's no problem. You can always agree to talk about one topic that day and the other the next time. Or you can split the time you scheduled into three parts and brainstorm about gratitude, your topic, and her topic. It is up to you how you manage the talk. If you have more than five people gathered, you might need to agree on one topic and schedule more meetings. Spending only a few minutes figuring the best solutions for issues is not enough. You won't get in-depth with any of the topics.

What matters is to always include gratitude, focus on what to do, not on what to avoid, seek the best solutions, avoid getting stuck in the problem, and be open with each other.

After a few weeks of practice you can introduce a new element into your conversation: as a cool down after the session you can share some good changes you experienced after the sessions. Talk about the consequences of implementing the best practices you figured during the sessions. Be totally objective. If something was unhelpful, go back to the topic and approach it from a different angle. If something your friend suggested brought some good results to you, mention it and thank her or him. Express your gratitude.

THE HOUR OF POWER AS AN INDIVIDUAL ACTIVITY

The main points of the Hour of Power as an individual activity are:

This type of HOP session, in some sense, is easier than the group activity version, since you don't have to compromise your time with anyone. You can practice it here and now, whenever you want. However, individual sessions lack the very thing that makes the HOP sessions special: shared growth. Still, if you can't synchronize a schedule with anyone, it is better to do it alone than not do it at all.

Let gratitude flood your heart. For those few minutes you choose to practice this exercise, think about things you are grateful for. Start with things about yourself, family, friends, workplace, and determinative events in your life. Feel gratitude for today because today is a gift. Commit to replacing your expectations with true gratitude, and optimistic thoughts for the future. Appreciate what you have. Trust that if you do your best, life will give you whatever is still missing. Don't get obsessed to get something—the less you care, the easier you'll achieve it.

If you're facing a problem, use top-down thinking. First, determine what the outcome is that you're wishing for. Then brainstorm backwards about the things you need to do to achieve it. Write down all the ideas that pop into your head, every good practice or solution that might help you achieve the desired outcome.

For example, do you want to double you income in a year? Then write down everything you need to do to achieve it. Let's say you make $5.000 per month now, but you want to make $10.000 within a year. Ground zero is $10.000, then. Write down everything you need to do to reach this goal. No negative thinking. No, "What if I don't make it?" Just put down everything you need to do to make that money. When you have a list of A-Z tasks, divide them to monthly goals, then weekly ones, than daily ones. Break up your big goal as much as you need to make it achievable.

10.000 dollars seems a big number to swallow. It means you have to make $333 a day (including Saturdays and Sundays). Does it still seem like a big number? Divide it into your working hours. Let's take the classic eight-hour workday. 333 divided by eight will make $41,7. You just need a job where you can make this amount per hour if you plan on working seven days a week, or you need a job where you can make double the amount per hour. A semi-good coach asks for $100-150 for an hour-long session. There you are. Now count how many clients you need. How frequently should they have sessions with you to achieve your monetary goal?

My example was just illustrative. There is something about it you might not have noticed—I never questioned the goal. I never said, "Meh, 10.000$ is impossible to reach." What I did was accept the goal and then brainstorm about different ways to reach it. This is what an individual HOP should be about: finding ways to reach whatever you want to reach not with complaining and expectations, but hands-on hard work.

Nothing worthwhile comes easy in life. Be grateful that you took the time to solely focus on life improvement instead of whining. You're doing your first, tenth, or one hundredth Hour of Power session, after all. In my experience, the best timing for individual HOP sessions are Sunday mornings. Then you're carefree, you don't have to work (if you're not a nine-to-five worker, choose a day which could be "Sunday" for you), and you don't feel pressured by obligations. Have an individual HOP session every Sunday, first to sort out plans for solving your problems, then to follow them up, and of course, to practice gratitude.

When you feel you've written enough on a session, take your voice recorder (the one you have on your phone is perfect) and read your points out loud. Listen to this recording multiple times a day. Also listen the recording in your next session.

Quick tip: for group HOPs you can also use the

recording practice. Write down the main ideas that come up after talking with your friends. When the session is over, read them out loud and record them so you can listen to it whenever you want as a reminder.

What are the benefits of the HOP sessions overall?

- Practice gratitude and let go of the toxic habit of stacking expectations;
- Create an automated idea machine for solving your problems and follow them up;
- Collect the best solutions to problems from your environment—get to know your loved ones and yourself better;
- Open up emotionally to your loved ones by sharing your goals and the things you feel grateful for;
- Develop a new, good routine in your life that has no risks or downside;
- Just chill, have fun, laugh, and spend quality time with people important to you (or just yourself).

The Hour of Power will gently kick you from your comfort zone, but in a pleasant way. It also trains your brain by challenging it in a positive direction. I really encourage you to try having an individual and group HOP. You've got nothing to lose but so much to gain.

If you take a liking to it, commit to scheduling sessions with the same frequency at the same time of day. Why is timing important? Did you ever order Blue Apron, Sun Basket, or any other home delivery food service? I have them deliver every week. One box comes on Tuesday, one on Friday. Those days are very special to me, and I always look forward to them, full of excitement over what will be in the box. The notion of having something to look forward to on those days makes me happy. There is magic in predictable positive events. The frenzy of looking forward to something sometimes is even better than the thing itself.

SUMMARY OF CHAPTER 4

1. The point of the Hour of Power is to jam into a gives session as much gratitude and constructive problem-solving ideas as possible.

2. The Hour of Power as a group activity: Agree on a goal you want to brainstorm about. This goal can be general to personal and you can divide the session into sections to cover them all. One segment of the session should be spent with sharing gratitude.

3. The Hour of Power as an individual activity: Think about what you wish to accomplish. Write down all the ideas that pop into your mind. Use top-down thinking. Don't even assume that the goal is unreachable. Record your ideas with a voice recorder so you can remind yourself about them later. One segment of the session should be about being grateful for what you have.

CHAPTER 5

THIRTY MINUTES FOR A HEALTHY BODY AND MIND

THE FIRST FIFTEEN MINUTES

I'm sure you've already made yourself a promise about start doing some exercises. You'll always start it tomorrow. Maybe you even pre-rewarded yourself with some crazy-expensive athletic attire to motivate yourself to keep your resolution. Even so, somehow the tomorrow never came, you had something going on every day and at the end of the day you pledged tomorrow will be different.

If you want a different outcome, you'll have to approach the problem differently.

First things first, you have to make time for exercise. You have to commit completely to the idea that for, let's not get too cocky with the time interval here, fifteen minutes you'll only do something related to motion. If you don't set your brain to that task, if you don't accept fully that this short period of time is reserved for physical activity, you'll find it is a time when you could do something else thus you'll start making excuses to avoid it. Commit to the idea of doing exercise in the morning for only a short period of time in the beginning.

Why should you do it? It is beneficial for your body and mind. Scientists who examined the correlation between the human body and mind in the 1920s proved that 30 percent of physical illnesses are rooted in inappropriate thinking. As the decades went on and more and more research was done, this percentage grew exponentially. Today most psychologists agree that almost 80 percent of physical illnesses originate with problems of mental health.

We can flip this coin. Mental activity has a direct connection to physical activity.

I'm sure you have had some days when you literally didn't do anything physical—apart from eating and other necessities. Maybe you got caught up in a Star Wars marathon or The Sims game trapped you in front of your computer. How did you feel that day? Fresh in mind and exploding from energy? I bet not. I bet you felt sluggish and mentally tired.

Conversely, how do you feel when you start your day with a short walk (maybe with your dog) in the morning? Or doing stretching exercise like morning yoga? Do you feel more awake and genuinely happier? Your answer would probably be yes.

One of reason for increased mental and physical awareness following some exercise is the release of serotonin in your body. This chemical is responsible for happiness, restful sleep, and a healthy appetite. It will help you feel more energized during the day, and you'll be able to think more clearly. Serotonin levels go up when you work out regularly. Low serotonin levels by contrast can lead to depression.

Regular exercise releases endorphins in your brain.

This hormone makes you happy and exhilarated, it can even lead to sports addiction in some people. This means that if you stop exercising for one reason or another, you might become moody.

Just like as I said with optimistic priming, start small. You don't have to start with the toughest fifteen-minute killer CrossFit workout. You can simply go for a walk or do some yoga at home. Or you can do as little as one pushup and a bit of walking.

The goal is to break out of your comfort zone, force yourself to take those first steps, and build up a new habit. You can always increase repetitions or time over time. But start with a small change.

Some people don't make changes because they think: what difference will one pushup make? It makes all the difference! It is a huge leap from nothing to something. There's always room for improvement. The first step is more about breaking that mental barrier than the pushup itself.

I exercise with music. When I wake up, after spending a few moments of gratitude, I put on my favorite music playlist and I start jumping around my room. Sometimes I sing and usually I make movements that would shame Will Ferrell in the movie A Night at the Roxbury, I can go quite hardcore. I wouldn't even call my practice "doing sports", rather just jumping around like a poisoned rabbit. Imagine doing a little workout to the Flash dance theme song—I bet it will fill you with energy. The crazier the things you do, the better you'll feel. Break your mental barriers, allow yourself to be silly. Adding a good laugh to your workout routine will double the benefits.

THE SECOND FIFTEEN MINUTES

Use the second fifteen minutes as a cool down after your workout. You can lie down in a relaxing yoga position. Lie on your back, spread your arms and legs a bit and feel how comfortable it is to relax after a physical effort. You deserve it. While you are lying in this position, listen to a meditation, or a podcast or an audiobook. If you're afraid that you might fall asleep, set the alarm on your phone for 15-20 minutes later.

If you don't want to lie down, that's fine too. You can sit down on a chair or go out to your porch. In this case you can listen to an audio book or read.

Here's a list of things you shouldn't listen to or read: don't read or listen to the news and don't mess with your emails or social media. Most successful people strongly recommend avoiding the online world for the first hour or two after you wake up. Just sit or lay down and listen to or read something that makes you happy and drives your day into a motivated zone.

When should you do these two fifteen-minute exercises?

Right after you wake up and spend a few moments with gratitude, jump out of the bed and start your crazy music workout or your chill yoga session. If you feel overly numb after waking up, you can start with the reading or listening exercise. I choose to do the physical exercise first to "eat that frog" first. But for some people it's a real challenge to do something physical after waking. Then just sit and read for a while. It's up to you.

I want to exclude the stress factor of time from

this exercise. If you don't have thirty minutes for the two, fifteen-minute-long exercise, simply do them ten - ten or five - five minutes. You can also play with the proportions: you can start with five - fifteen minute exercises—where you do sports for five minutes and read for fifteen or vice versa. It is better to leave room for improvement and set achievable goals in the beginning.

SUMMARIZING CHAPTER 5

1. You have to commit totally to the thought that in those fifteen minutes you'll do nothing but exercise.
2. Today most psychologists agree that the cause of almost 80 percent of physical illnesses originates with mental health.
3. Regular exercise causes your brain to release endorphins. This hormone makes you feel happy and exhilarated. It can even lead to exercise addiction in some people.
4. Start small, do it with music.

5. Sit down in a chair or go out to your porch to read. The book should be motivational. Don't read news or emails.

6. If you don't have thirty minutes for the exercises, do them in twenty or ten minutes.

CHAPTER 6

OTHERS' BEST PRACTICES

In this chapter, I share the morning habits, practices, and rules of some of the most successful people in the world. I'd like to emphasize that you shouldn't try to introduce all of them into your life, especially not all at once. These practices serve the purpose of offering you a variety of options, in case you didn't find anything valuable until now in this book.

This chapter will show what billionaires, best selling authors, top musicians, and successful actors do differently. The way they live their lives largely contributes to what they achieve.

Let's start with Tony Robbins, a world famous motivational speaker and best-selling author. He has regular morning routines in his life. He rightfully says that if you "don't have ten minutes in your day for yourself then you don't have a life." In his morning routine he listens to motivational music. He also does breathing exercises taking deep breaths to change his physical and mental condition. Unsurprisingly, with his level of consciousness he knows the importance of gratitude in life. He focuses on gratitude for at least three minutes. He also prays for his family and friends for a few minutes. Finally repeats the top three things he wants to accomplish for the day.

Mr. Robbins has his own Hour of Power, or 30 minutes to thrive, or 15 minutes of fulfillment practices. To find out more about them check out his Peak Performance 60 program. Mr. Robbins' other morning routines include jumping in a hot and cold pool, meditating, or running on a treadmill.

Tony Robbins may not be the best example since it is his job to be highly motivated and positive. He has to set a proper example.

The morning habits of one of the most influential

people of the world, the former president of the United States, Barack Obama were probably different now than they were during his presidency.

When he was still a president, he woke up two hours before his first appointment of the day. Mr. Obama started his day with an intensive 45-minute workout. Facing a lot of pressure during his presidency, he needed to release stress. After the workout he had a healthy breakfast. He believes a good breakfast can help keep up his energy for the rest of the day. He avoids coffee but drinks water, fresh orange juice, or green tea.

Another thing Mr. Obama avoided and probably still avoids in his first two hours after waking up is criticism. He excluded the news and media from his morning routine. As a world leader, he received a lot of good and bad every day—it makes sense that he needed a break from them. He is a human being just like the rest of us, and just like us he's not immune to tragedies, blaming, ugly words and so on.

One of the most well-known empowering question comes from Steve Jobs, co- founder, chairman, and CEO of Apple Inc. Mr. Jobs asked himself this every morning: *if today was the last day of my life, would I do what I am about to do?* If the answer was "no" for a few days in a row, he changed his plans and schedule.

What a powerful statement! Imagine how difficult it is to admit that what you are doing day after day is not worthy of your time. Do you have the guts to change it? That's the real challenge. You may argue that what Steve Jobs could do easily, we normal folks can't. We can't just leave our jobs if we observe that it steals away our life. That's true. But don't forget that Steve Jobs had problems too, just like you and me—it's just that his problems were better than ours. Whatever changes he made in his life were still a sacrifice. Throwing away your job just because it's not your dream career is not a smart step, if you do it suddenly. If, however, you just acknowledge this fact and make small changes to get rid of the job eventually, the transition will make you much happier. The hope of getting out of the rat race and the conscious steps made toward this goal will keep your spirits high.

If there is a repeated and despised part of your day,

and you can skip it or leave it, you should. If you cannot skip it without significant consequences that would cause you more harm than good, find an activity that minimizes the damage caused by the unpleasant event.

For example, you hate your colleague, but you have to deal with her because you sit next to each other and can't change your place in the office. Without quitting your job you can't escape her. If you were to quit your job, you'd risk pushing yourself into an unstable financial situation that could cause you a great deal of anxiety. Do not quit in this case because the benefits are not worth the price. Better start studying something else on the weekends or save an hour each day to search for another job in the same field. You'll realize you have many other options. One day you'll be able to quit, risk free. In the meantime, you channeled your negative energy generated by the annoying colleague into a plan for a better life.

If today was the last day of your life, what would you do? The same as you plan to do today?

Mark Zuckerberg, co-founder and CEO of Facebook, wears the same type of shirt every morning. He made this decision to escape decision fatigue. Making so many decisions every day makes him tired so he simplifies the non-important decisions as much as possible.

Bill Gates, one of the richest people in the world, spends one hour on the treadmill every morning while he watches videos from the Teaching Company.

Ben Franklin woke up at 4:00 a.m. regularly. He actively practiced positive thinking by asking himself what good he could do that day?

Richard Branson, the founder of Virgin American Airlines, has a morning practice that would be quite challenging for many of us. He swims around his island. He does, however, a much more mundane morning routine, too. He plays tennis before breakfast.

Mick Jagger, the lead singer of Rolling Stones, works out six days a week to reduce stress. He is 73 years old, by the way, and still rolling.

If you're thinking that only middle-aged to older men have good morning habits, you're wrong. Lady Gaga, the famous American singer and actress, does yoga every morning. She also practices five minutes of self-directed love in an effort to stand tall and overcome challenging times.

Last but not least, here's the routine of Stephen King, the best horror and supernatural fiction author of our time, wakes up at around 8:00 a.m. He sits for a half an hour, drinks water or orange juice, and listens to music. This practice helps him clear his mind and get into the zone to write engaging stories.

As you can see, even the most successful people use different morning routines. These routines may vary in the terms of waking hour, length of the practice, or the place of the practice. Some common features, however, can be extracted from them. Almost all the aforementioned people have some type of physical exercise integrated into their routine, some mental wake-up activity, and a short period of practicing gratitude. They also have a desire to simplify unimportant decisions (like what to wear), and exclude negativity from their morning (like the news).

Most people say waking up early is the key to a successful start of the day. In Hungary we have a saying, "He who wakes up early finds gold." It is an old folk locution and there must be a good reason why it survived through the centuries.

SUMMARIZING CHAPTER 6

1. If you, "don't have ten minutes in your day for yourself then you don't have a life."
2. A good breakfast can keep up your energy for the rest of the day.
3. If today was the last day of your life, would you do what you are about to do?
4. Simplify the unimportant decisions as much as possible.
5. Practice five minutes of self-directed love to stand tall and overcome challenging times.

CHAPTER 7

MORNING NUTRITION AND HEALTH

DON'T GET SHORT ON ENERGY

Everyone is short on time. We stress about how our time is limited here, our time is limited there. But there is something that is even more limited than our time and we tend to forget about it. It is our energy.

You have to lay the foundation of an energized body in the morning to establish a good energy level for the rest of the day.

We start with a certain energy level when we wake up. For somebody who wakes up between 7 and 8 a.m., the high-energy zone will last until 11 a.m. under normal circumstances. After that, the energy level will decrease.

I call this the 7/11 rule: wake up at 7 a.m. and do your most important tasks in that high-energy zone that lasts until 11:00 a.m.

Nutrition influences a lot how much energy you have during the day. The average person is careless after wake up. They don't eat breakfast or eat only a small amount. Then around noon, they eat a huge lunch and knock themselves out energetically for at least two hours.

Why are they tired? Two reasons. First, because they start digesting like an anaconda after eating a crocodile. The brain is busy digesting the crocodile so unless crocodile digestion is your primary goal, you're not helping yourself with that big lunch. Second, because the human circadian rhythm has the greatest desire to sleep in the middle of the night, between 2 a.m. and 3 a.m., about twelve hours later, between 2 p.m. and 3 p.m. you can experience a short period of sleepiness. If this coincides with your post-lunch energy dip the cumulative effect can easily make you drowsy.

How can you develop healthy energy management habits that start when you wake up?

MAKE AN ENERGY JOURNAL

Take a week to monitor your energy fluctuation. This means you need to, on an hourly basis, pay attention to how energized you feel. Ten is very energized, one is on the verge of sleep. Log this in a journal every hour beginning with the hour you wake up and ending with the hour you go to sleep. It's a bit fussy, but you only have to do it once.

Don't change anything in your routine while you monitor, just take notes about everything you experience to identify which periods of the day you feel most energized. You'll be surprised by the discoveries you make. If you follow the same eating and sleeping schedule, you'll see that your most energetic periods fall on the same hours every day.

After you've identified your high, medium, and low energy level times, you'll know how to arrange your daily tasks to maximize your productivity potential. The most important tasks should be done in the high-energy periods, and the low priority tasks in the low-energy periods.

When you decide to change your life, you want to change everything, your behavior, habits, health habits, attitude toward your relationship. Everything. But if you change all of these things, you'll end up not changing anything because you won't be able to respect and adjust to all these sudden changes.

Do not rush. Start with small changes and remember, do not change more than three things at a time. If your primary goal is to introduce healthy nutrition as a morning habit, focus on this.

How long does it take to make a new practice a habit?

Dr. Maxwell Maltz, a plastic surgeon, concluded that patients need 21 days to recover and get used to the changes after a plastic surgery. He popularized the concept that breaking a habit and replacing it with another also takes 21 days. However, a study from the University Collage London proved that the number of days might vary between 18 and 254 depending on the individual and the change. In my opinion something becomes a habit when you don't have to focus on doing it anymore.

You have to be conscious of your sleeping and eating habits. In the long term a complete lifestyle change will be necessary if right now you live like a wild horse, on four hours sleep and ramen. Here are some of the most important health improvements you could make:

Sleep at least seven hours.

"Eat breakfast like a king, lunch like a prince, and dinner like a pauper." This quote comes from the famous nutritionist, Adele Davis. I highly recommend her books as a guide to lifestyle change. After reading her studies you'll know you should have a copious breakfast, a moderate lunch, and a small dinner. In his Phoenix seminar, Brian Tracy, entrepreneur, professional speaker and bestselling author, states that we should consume 80 percent of our daily calories before 2:00 p.m. to maximize achievement and balance weight control.

Avoid the "white poisons," like sugar, flour, salt, and milk.

When it comes to carbs, the more complex the better. Stick to vegetables or whole grains that contain lots of fiber. Refined carbohydrates, like sugary foods, are not your friends.

Help your digestive system by combining foods in a way that makes them easier for your stomach to digest. Do not eat proteins with starches. Proteins require an acid medium for digestion. This acid neutralizes the alkaline medium necessary for starch digestion. Thus, you will end up with indigestion from fermentation. You'll feel heavy and exhausted.[3]

The top nutritionists around the world say starches, green vegetables, sugars, and fat can be eaten together. They need either an alkaline or neutral medium for digestion. Proteins, acid fruits, and green vegetables can also be eaten together as they require an acid or neutral medium for digestion. Starches and proteins as well as acid fruits and fats shouldn't be combined in a meal if you want easy digestion.[4]

Proper energy management takes a lot of attention and persistence, but is worth going an extra mile for it. Not only will you have a healthier lifestyle, but also your energy level will be more stable. Of all the body's internal functions, digestion requires the most energy. If you can minimize it, lots of useful energy will be liberated to be used to do something more meaningful in your life.

To have well-balanced energy management and to get the maximum benefit from your energy, you should follow the advice above throughout the day not just in the morning.

MORNING HEALTH ROUTINES

Having healthy skin, explosive energy, and looking refreshed when starting the day are things everyone—men and women—want.

Karl Lagerfeld, the creative designer of Chanel said, "Beauty—or the desire to be beautiful—is in itself a dangerous motivation. So don't focus on beauty... a respectable appearance is sufficient to make people more interested in your soul." And "respectable appearance" can be many things: an energetic and happy personality, a glowing, healthy skin, or a fit body.

The following morning health routines are simple

practices that can help you feel and look better, and be healthier.

HYDRATE

Drink a tall glass of water in the morning. If you slept seven to eight hours it means you didn't drink any fluids in that time. Water hydrates you, fires up your metabolism, cleans your body of toxins, gives your brain fuel, and even helps you eat less. Your body contains at least 70 percent water—you need to consume water in order to stay healthy.

Alternatively, you can choose to drink warm water with a bit of freshly squeezed lemon juice. Warm water won't shock your system as much as cold will first thing in the morning. The lemon will add a nice flavor and help get your digestive system ready for breakfast.

PRO-BREAKFAST

Eat most of your daily protein in the morning. A study in the *International Journal of Obesity* shows that eating protein in the morning can improve your appetite control, which can result in consuming up to 400 fewer calories throughout the day.[5] People often eat breakfasts rich in carbs and fat. But this is not as satisfying as a breakfast rich in protein. Researchers at the University of Missouri-Columbia conducted an experiment involving people between the age 18-55. Those who ate a protein-rich breakfast (containing 30-39 grams of protein) ate a smaller lunch.[6]

PRO-WEIGHT LOSS

If loosing weight is one of your main goals, you can start working toward it in the morning by raising the amount of protein in your body. A study done by Authority Nutrition shows that eating more protein can boost your metabolic rate—burn more calories and reduce your appetite. Protein, which should make up around 25-30 percent of your calories, has been shown to boost metabolism by up to 80 or even 100 calories per day, compared to lower protein diets. This study was supported by the National Center for Biotechnology Information.[7]

PRO-FUN

For fun I've included the link to a protein calculator. Based on age, height, weight, fitness, and nutrition goals, it calculates the daily amount of protein you should consume. Check out the calculator on the following link: http://www.bodybuilding.com/fun/bbprotein.htm.

COFFEE VS. GREEN TEA

Many people debate which of these drinks is better for your health, which gives you more energy, which contains more vitamins and anti-oxidants. *Medical Daily* published a study on the benefits and risks of both. Let's take a quick look at the pros and cons of coffee and green tea.

Coffee: it was discovered much later than the tea. The most common origin theory is that coffee was first discovered in the Ethiopian highlands, where a goat herder noticed his goats became hyperactive after eating certain berries. Later, monks in monasteries used coffee to help them stay alert while praying. For a long time coffee was known only in the eastern world and it was not common in Europe until the 17th century.

Since then a lot of research has been done on the benefits and risks of coffee. Vague connections have been made between coffee consumption and the reduction of dementia, Alzheimer's, and type 2 diabetes. And since coffee has a higher amount of caffeine than tea, it can constrict blood vessels in the brain and reducing migraines or the symptoms of hangovers. Coffee contains essential nutrients such as riboflavin (vitamin B2), pantothenic acid (vitamin B5), manganese, potassium, magnesium, and niacin (Vitamin B3). Although all these essentials can be found only in small dosages in a cup of coffee (3-11% of the RDA) for those who drink several cups of coffee a day, it can add up.

However, a study from Harvard's School of Public Health concluded that coffee is a "neutral" drink, having neither a great health benefit nor harmful effect.

(Green) Tea: the origins of the discovery of tea goes back much farther in history than coffee. It's said that tea was discovered in 2737 BC by the Emperor of China while he was boiling water under a tree. The leaves of the tree fell into the water and when the emperor drank it, he found the taste to be very pleasant. Tea has been associated with meditation, mindfulness, and spirituality since it was first used by priests and scholars of East Asia.

A few thousand years later the National Cancer Institute proved that tealeaves contain an anti-oxidant called polyphenol, which can help prevent cancer. After being cut, tealeaves go through an oxidation process, which determines the amount of polyphenol contained in each type of tea. Not all types of tea have the same amount of anti-oxidants. Green tea has one of the highest levels of polyphenol and thus the highest beneficial effects. Also, teas with the highest levels of polyphenols are usually brewed hot rather than cold or ice teas.

As for cons, over-consuming anything that contains caffeine—coffee and tea—can result in increased anxiety, heart palpitations, insomnia, and restlessness. Large amounts of unfiltered coffee have been linked to higher levels of bad cholesterol. Also, tea contains fluoride and too much fluoride, while good for your teeth, may increase your risk of brittle bones. Some tea blends from

China, India, and Sri Lanka have been found to contain aluminum and lead. So make sure you get your tea from a safe source.

All in all, drinking one or the other in the morning can help you feel less tired, and improve your physical performance by increasing adrenaline in your blood.

Since it is debatable whether you should drink caffeine in the morning or at all, I won't hit the table with frothing mouth and bloody eyes and demand that you do it. I summed up the research and I concluded that (unless you suffer from a health condition that prohibits you from drinking caffeine) as long as you don't over- consume caffeine, you'll be fine.[8]

DRY BRUSH YOUR BODY

Dry brushing your body helps improve your circulation and remove dead skin cells. Brushing from your extremities toward your heart is essential. Cover all of your parts before hopping into the shower. Besides the physiological benefits, this practice will leave your skin feeling smoother. Apply moisturizer after your shower to retain that suppleness. An exfoliating brush like a dry loofah, which should not be too rough, is the best choice you can make. Don't go for the softest brush because it won't do the job, but if you opt for a softer brush you can apply more pressure while using it so as to exfoliate your skin in the right amount.

SUMMARY OF CHAPTER 7

1. Take a week to monitor your energy fluctuation. This means you need to pay attention to how you feel on an hourly basis.
2. Do not change more than three things at the time.
3. Help your digestive system by combining foods in a way that makes them easier for your stomach to digest.
4. Drink a tall glass of water in the morning. If you sleep seven to eight hours that means you didn't drink any fluids in that time.
5. Eat a high amount of protein in the morning.

6. Drinking green tea or coffee in the morning can help you feel less tired, and it improves physical performance by increasing adrenaline in your blood.
7. Dry brushing the body helps improve your circulation and removes dead skin cells.

CLOSING WORDS

I want to tell you one last thing before I let you go start practicing these new exercises: Do not stress! Do not stress over making these changes. Stress kills success. The more you care and stress about something the lower the chances that you're actually going to succeed. You don't make changes in your life because you must. You make them to feel better, to live better and be happier—whatever that means to you.

Don't stress yourself out more than you already are, choose a maximum of three things to change and be patient with yourself. You'll make mistakes. Especially in the beginning when you forget or simply don't want to do what you signed up for. As long as not doing doesn't become a habit, you're on board and you're going to be fine.

I believe in you!

Yours truly,

Zoe

P.S.: If you have questions please don't hesitate to contact me on **zoemckey@gmail.com**. I welcome any kind of constructive opinion as well. I'd like to know how I can help so please share your ideas with me. If you'd like to get helpful tips from me on a weekly basis, visit me at **www.zoemckey.com** and subscribe. Thank you!

REFERENCE

Books:

Goleman, Daniel. *Emotional Intelligence*. London: Bloomsbury. 2010

Kahneman, D., & Tversky, A. *Prospect theory: An analysis of decision under risk*. pg. 47, 263-291. Econometrica. 1979.

Manson, Mark. *The subtle art of not giving a f*ck*. Strawberry Hills, NSW: ReadHowYouWant, 2017.

Websites:

Bushak, Lecia. *Health Benefits Of Coffee vs. Tea: Which One Is Better For You?*

Medical Daily. 2014. http://www.medicaldaily.com/health-benefits-coffee-vs-tea- which-one-better-you-309556 (accessed September 30, 2016)

Dr. Kaslow. *Food Combining*. Dr. Kaslow. 2006. http://www.drkaslow.com/html/food_combining.html (accessed September 27, 2016)

Farley, Amy. *How to Use Food as a Jet Lag Cure*. Travel+Leisure. http://www.travelandleisure.com/blogs/food-as-a-jet-lag-cure (accessed October 4, 2016)

Gunnars, Kris. *How Protein Can Help You Lose Weight Naturally*. Authority Nutrition. 2015. https://authoritynutrition.com/how-protein-can-help-you-lose-weight/ (accessed September 30, 2016)

International Journal of Obesity. *Short Communication*. Nature. 2015. http://www.nature.com/ijo/journal/v39/n9/full/ijo2015101a.html (accessed October 1, 2016)

Logan, Gaby. *How Long Does it Take to Get Over Jet Lag?* USA Today. http://traveltips.usatoday.com/long-over-jet-lag-63114.html (accessed October 7, 2016)

Manson, Mark. *How To Make Your Own Luck*. Mark Manson. 2012. https://markmanson.net/how-to-make-your-own-luck (accessed October 4, 2016)

Raw Food Explained. *Digestive Physiology And Food Combining*. Raw Food

Explained. 2006. http://www.rawfoodexplained.com/digestive-physiology-and-food-combining/food-combining-rules.html (accessed September 27, 2016)

Starek Joanna E. & Keating, Caroline F.. *Self-Deception and Its Relationship to Success in Competition.* Taylor&Francis Online. 2010. http://www.tandfonline.com/doi/abs/10.1207/s15324834basp1202_2 (accessed September 14, 2016)

University of Missouri-Columbia. *Protein-rich breakfast helps curb appetite throughout the morning.* ScienceDaily. www.sciencedaily.com/releases/2013/11/131114102528.htm (accessed October 10, 2016)

ENDNOTES

1. Amy Farley. *How to Use Food as a Jet Lag Cure.* Travel+Leisure. http://www.travelandleisure.com/blogs/food-as-a-jet-lag-cure (accessed October 4, 2016)
2. Gaby Logan. *How Long Does it Take to Get Over Jet Lag?* USA Today. http://traveltips.usatoday.com/long-over-jet-lag-63114.html (accessed October 7, 2016)
3. Dr. Kaslow. *Food Combining.* Dr. Kaslow. 2006. http://www.drkaslow.com/html/food_combining.html (accessed September 27, 2016)
4. Raw Food Explained. *Digestive Physiology And Food Combining.* Raw Food Explained. 2006. http://www.rawfoodexplained.com/digestive-physiology-and-food-combining/food-combining-rules.html (accessed September 27, 2016)

5. International Journal of Obesity. *Short Communication*. Nature. 2015. http://www.nature.com/ijo/journal/v39/n9/full/ijo2015101a.html (accessed October 1, 2016)

6. University of Missouri-Columbia. *Protein-rich breakfast helps curb appetite throughout the morning.* ScienceDaily. www.sciencedaily.com/releases/2013/11/131114102528.htm (accessed October 10, 2016)

7. Kris Gunnars. *How Protein Can Help You Lose Weight Naturally.* Authority Nutrition. 2015. https://authoritynutrition.com/how-protein-can-help-you-lose-weight/ (accessed September 30, 2016)

8. Lecia Bushak. *Health Benefits Of Coffee vs. Tea: Which One Is Better For You?.* Medical Daily. 2014. http://www.medicaldaily.com/health-benefits-coffee-vs-tea-which-one-better-you-309556 (accessed September 30, 2016)